THE PLANETS OF OUR SOLAR SYSTEM

PLUTO AND THE DWARF PLANETS

by Sue Bradford Edwards

BrightPoint Press

San Diego, CA

BrightPoint Press

an imprint of ReferencePoint Press, Inc.
Printed in the United States

For more information, contact:
BrightPoint Press
PO Box 27779
San Diego, CA 92198
www.BrightPointPress.com

LIBRARY OF CONGRESS CATALOGING-IN-PUBLICATION DATA

Name: Edwards, Sue Bradford, author.
Title: Pluto and the Dwarf Planets / by Sue Bradford Edwards.
Description: San Diego, CA: ReferencePoint Press, 2026 | Series: The planets of our solar system | Audience: Grade 7 to 9 | Includes bibliographical references and index.
Identifiers: ISBN: 9781678211707 (hardcover) | ISBN: 9781678211714 (eBook)
The complete Library of Congress record is available at www.loc.gov.

CONTENTS

AT A GLANCE

- In 2006, the International Astronomical Union defined what a planet is. Under the new definition, some objects in space formerly considered planets were now considered dwarf planets.

- The gravity of a dwarf planet is not strong enough to clear the dwarf planet's orbital path of other objects.

- Ceres is the only dwarf planet that has been discovered in the solar system's asteroid belt. The dwarf planets Pluto, Haumea, Makemake, Quaoar, and Eris are located in the Kuiper Belt beyond Neptune.

- Many of the dwarf planets in the solar system have moons.

- Pluto has five known moons. Its largest is called Charon.

- Ceres was the first dwarf planet to be discovered in the solar system. Italian astronomer Giuseppe Piazzi saw it through a telescope in 1801.
- Pluto was discovered in 1930 by American astronomer Clyde Tombaugh.
- The Hubble Space Telescope (HST) orbits Earth. Astronomers have used it to learn more about dwarf planets and their moons.
- The first spacecraft to visit a dwarf planet was called *Dawn*. It went into orbit around Ceres in 2015.
- The *New Horizons* spacecraft flew by Pluto and its moons in 2015.

SEEING CERES

In March 2015, a spacecraft called *Dawn* reached the dwarf planet Ceres. The spacecraft had been launched in 2007 by the National Aeronautics and Space Administration (NASA). *Dawn* orbited Ceres. It captured images of the dwarf planet. It sent the images back to scientists on Earth.

The scientists noticed something in the images of Ceres. They saw bright spots in a crater named Occator. One spot

***Dawn* was launched into space aboard a Delta 2925H rocket.**

USAF
ULA
DELTA

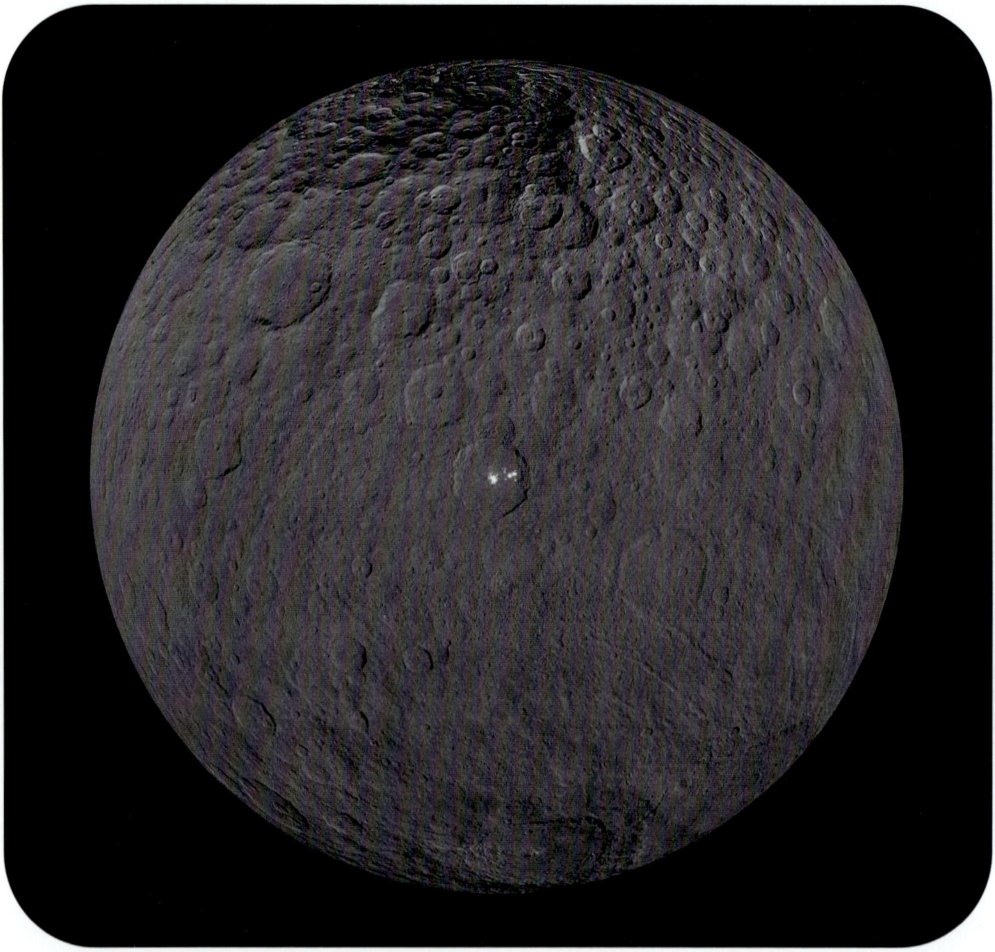

Occator is named after a Roman agricultural god.

was in a low place in the crater's center. The scientists studied these light areas. They were salts on the surface of the dwarf planet.

The presence of these salts taught scientists about Ceres's past.

They suspected that a space rock had struck Ceres about 20 million years ago. The impact formed Occator. It also heated that area of Ceres. Salty ice below the surface melted. This created a brine. A brine is a mixture of liquid water and salt. The water seeped onto the surface. Then it **evaporated**. It left the salt behind. This created the white spots that *Dawn* discovered.

Scientists were excited to learn these details about Ceres's past. They continued to study *Dawn*'s images of the dwarf planet. But the spacecraft could not produce new images forever. By late October 2018, it ran out of fuel. Scientists received no more signals from *Dawn*. The scientists were happy with what they had learned.

NASA scientist Marc Rayman says, "*Dawn* accomplished far more than we hoped."[1]

DISTANT WORLDS

The solar system's dwarf planets are smaller than its eight planets. Most are

After *Dawn* ran out of fuel, it remained in orbit around Ceres. NASA scientists expected the spacecraft to orbit for at least 20 more years, and likely decades more.

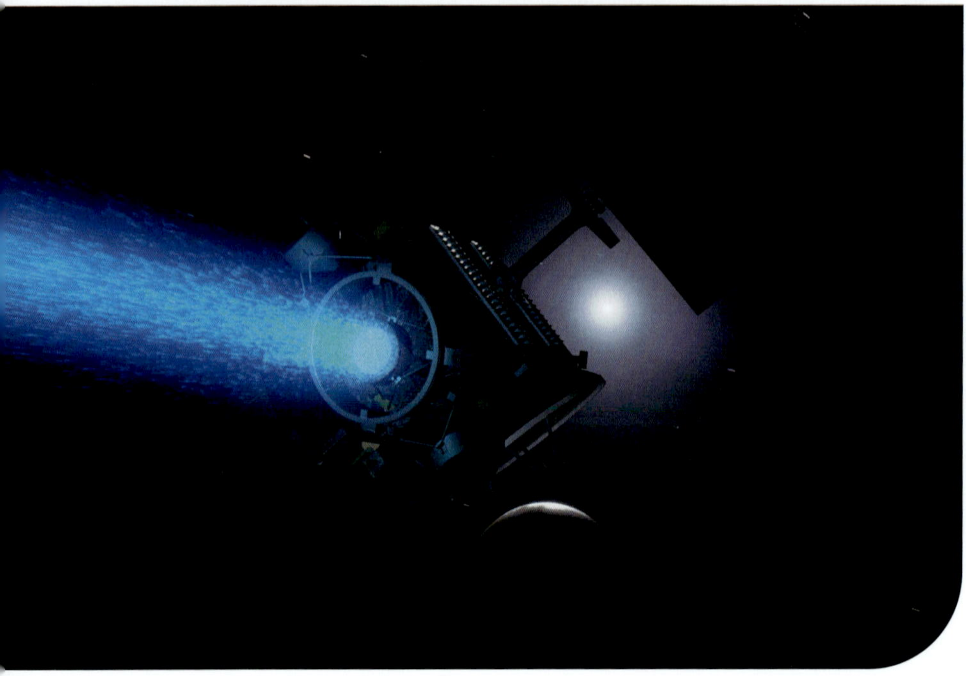

very far from Earth. This makes studying them difficult. Ceres is hundreds of millions of miles from Earth. Before the invention of spaceflight, people could only observe dwarf planets from Earth. They used telescopes. People discovered some dwarf planets using telescopes. But they struggled to study dwarf planets in detail.

The invention of spaceflight changed everything. Scientists could send spacecraft beyond Earth. Now people could learn more about distant objects, including the dwarf planets.

CHAPTER ONE

THE DWARF PLANETS

In 2006, the International **Astronomical** Union (IAU) defined what a planet is. The definition had three parts. A planet must orbit a star. It must be round or nearly round. And no objects of similar size can be in its orbital path.

Dwarf planets are like planets. They orbit a star. They are round or nearly round. But they share their orbits with objects of similar size. Their gravity is not strong enough to

Although there are many small objects in its orbital path, Jupiter is considered a planet because none of those objects is anywhere close in size to Jupiter.

Pluto is considered a dwarf planet because it has not cleared its orbit of objects of similar size.

remove these objects. “They don’t clear out a gap,” says Dr. Phil Sutton.[2]

The IAU officially recognized five dwarf planets as of February 2025. Ceres orbits between Mars and Jupiter in the asteroid belt. Pluto, Makemake, Haumea, and Eris are in the Kuiper Belt. This belt is beyond Neptune. The IAU also referred to an object called Quaoar as a dwarf planet in a report, but did not officially recognize it as one elsewhere. Other scientists and institutions recognize additional dwarf planets. And there may be more than a hundred undiscovered dwarf planets in the solar system.

IN THE ASTEROID BELT

Asteroids are rocky objects that orbit the Sun. The asteroid belt is a dense band of asteroids between Mars and Jupiter. Some of the largest objects in the asteroid belt are dwarf planets. These include Ceres.

Ceres orbits 257 million miles (413 million km) from the Sun on average. Its distance from the Sun makes it much colder than Earth. Daytime temperatures vary from –136°F to –28°F (–93°C to –33°C). Ceres is about 592 miles (952 km) in diameter. Its mass is about 1 percent of that of Earth's Moon.

It takes Ceres 1,682 Earth days to circle the Sun. It spins on its **axis of rotation** once every 9 hours. This means a day on Ceres is 9 hours long. Ceres spins nearly upright in relation to its orbit around

At Ceres's average distance from the Sun, sunlight takes 22 minutes to reach the dwarf planet.

Ceres is covered with many small craters.

the Sun. Its axis is tilted by only 4 degrees. When an object's axis is very tilted, some parts receive more sunlight than other parts at certain times. This creates seasons. Ceres's nearly upright axis means it has no distinct seasons.

Ceres has a very thin **atmosphere**. It contains water vapor. This water may burst onto the surface from inside Ceres. Or it may come from melting ice near the planet's surface. Ceres is mostly rocky. Ceres's salts are not like table salt. They are made of different chemicals.

THE KUIPER BELT

The Kuiper Belt lies beyond Neptune. It is doughnut shaped. It is made up of objects known as Kuiper Belt Objects (KBOs). KBOs include asteroids, **comets**, and dwarf planets. Scientists believe these objects were left over when the outer planets formed. The outer planets are Jupiter, Saturn, Uranus, and Neptune.

The dwarf planet Pluto is in the Kuiper Belt. It orbits about 3.7 billion miles (5.9 billion km) from the Sun on average. Its orbit is oval shaped instead of circular. Pluto can be as close as 2.8 billion miles

Mountain ranges and flatlands are visible in this picture of Pluto's surface.

(4.5 billion km) from the Sun. At other times, it is 4.6 billion miles (7.4 billion km) from the Sun. Pluto is very cold. Its average temperature is –387°F (–232°C).

Pluto is 1,477 miles (2,377 km) in diameter. Its mass is about one-sixth of the mass of Earth's Moon. Pluto takes 248 years to circle the Sun. Each day on Pluto is about 153 hours long. The dwarf planet's axis is tilted by 57 degrees. At its center, Pluto has a rocky core surrounded by a layer of water ice and other frozen substances. Pluto's surface has landforms also found on Earth. These include plains, mountains, and valleys. Pluto also has many craters.

Haumea is another dwarf planet in the Kuiper Belt. It orbits about 4 billion miles (6.5 billion kilometers) from the Sun on average. The average temperature is –400°F (–240°C). Haumea is encircled by

Tenzing Montes

The Tenzing Montes are Pluto's tallest mountains. They are about 3.7 miles (6 km) tall. They were named after Tenzing Norgay. Norgay guided explorers in the Himalayan Mountains in Asia. In 1953, Norgay and New Zealander explorer Edmund Hilary became the first to top Mount Everest, the tallest mountain on Earth.

a ring. Scientists know little about Haumea's atmosphere or landforms.

Haumea is oval shaped. It is about 1,430 miles (2,300 km) wide on its longest side. Its mass is about 5 percent of that of Earth's Moon. Haumea's axis tilts by about 28 degrees. Haumea takes 285 Earth years to orbit the Sun. It spins once every

This illustration shows Haumea's rings, which were the first to be discovered orbiting a KBO.

4 hours. This means Haumea has one of the shortest days in the solar system.

Scientists suggest that something large may have hit Haumea billions of years ago. The strike could have created its two moons. They are called Namaka and Hi‘aka. The strike could also have caused Haumea's rapid spin.

The dwarf planet Makemake is also in the Kuiper Belt. It orbits about 4.3 billion miles (6.8 billion km) from the Sun on average. Makemake takes 305 years to circle the Sun. It rotates once every 22 and a half hours. This means its day is similar in length to a day on Earth.

Makemake's average temperature is –405.5°F (–243°C). This dwarf planet is about 888 miles (1430 km) in diameter.

Quaoar's ring and moon appear in this illustration of the dwarf planet.

Its mass is 4.2 percent of the Earth's Moon. Scientists do not know much about its surface.

Quaoar is also in the Kuiper Belt. This dwarf planet orbits about 4 billion miles (6.5 billion km) from the Sun on average. It takes 283.6 years to circle the Sun. Its day is 17.7 hours long. Its axis is tilted by 8 degrees.

Scientists suspect Quaoar's temperature is about –364°F (–220°C). The dwarf planet is about 677 miles (1,090 km) in diameter on average. Scientists think Quaoar is coated in water ice. Like Haumea, it has a ring.

Eris is another dwarf planet in the Kuiper Belt. It orbits about 6.3 billion miles (10 billion km) from the Sun on average. It takes 557 years to circle the Sun. It rotates once every 25.9 hours. This means its days are slightly longer than Earth's. Eris's axis is tilted by 44 degrees.

Scientists suspect that Eris's average temperature is about –382°F (–230°C). The dwarf planet is 1,500 miles (2,400 km) in diameter. Its mass is about 22 percent of that of Earth's Moon. Eris may have a rocky surface like Pluto. When Eris is far from the Sun, material in its atmosphere freezes. It falls to the surface as snow.

WHERE THE DWARF PLANETS ORBIT

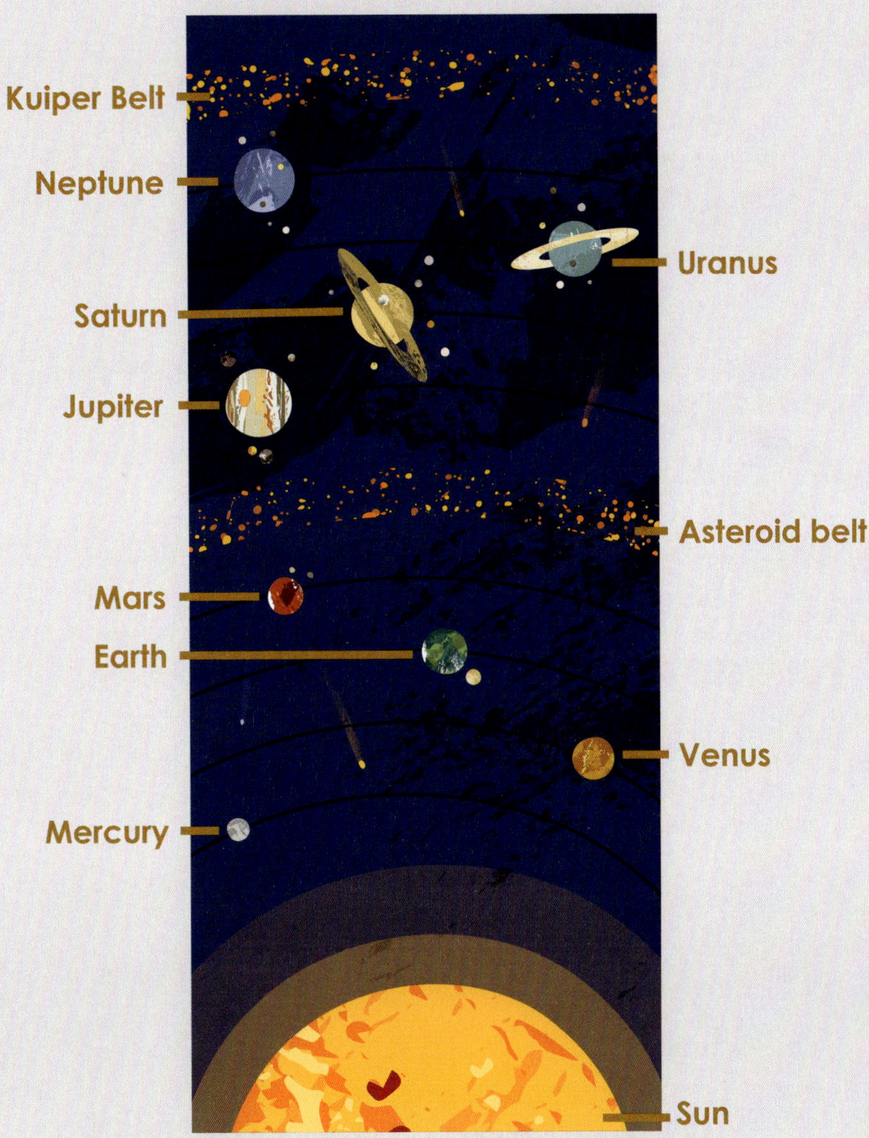

The solar system's two main belts are the asteroid belt and the Kuiper Belt. Ceres orbits in the asteroid belt, while Eris, Haumea, Pluto, Makemake, and Quaoar orbit in the Kuiper Belt.

CHAPTER TWO

DISCOVERING THE DWARF PLANETS

The first astronomers studied space by looking up at the sky. Many stars and planets are visible in the night sky. But the dwarf planets are too small and too distant to be seen by the naked eye.

The invention of the telescope in the early 1600s changed everything. Astronomers used telescopes to discover many new objects in the sky. They also used them to learn more about the objects people had

Early telescopes inspired the creation of modern telescopes that astronomers use to study space today.

already discovered. It was only a matter of time before telescopes helped people discover the first dwarf planet.

Gazing through a telescope in 1801, Italian astronomer Giuseppe Piazzi discovered Ceres. It was the first object identified in the asteroid belt. Piazzi thought Ceres was an asteroid. He named it Ceres after the Roman goddess of harvests and corn. Ceres was not recognized as a dwarf planet until 2006.

DISCOVERING PLUTO

American astronomer Clyde Tombaugh discovered Pluto in 1930. He did so at the Lowell **Observatory** in Flagstaff, Arizona. A device called a blink comparator helped him discover the dwarf planet. First, Tombaugh

Giuseppe Piazzi was born in Italy on July 16, 1746.

took multiple photographs of the same region of the night sky at different times. Then he loaded the photographs into the blink comparator. This device allowed him to switch between two images very quickly.

Tombaugh's blink comparator could switch between images several times per second.

He was looking for objects that moved between the time he took one photograph and the next. Eventually, he noticed a new moving object. That object turned out to be Pluto.

At first, Pluto was considered the ninth planet in the solar system. But by the 1990s, people had discovered similarly sized objects in the Kuiper Belt. These objects called into question the definition of a planet. In 2006, the IAU defined what a planet is more precisely. Pluto did not meet this definition. Instead, it was a dwarf planet. But it was still interesting to scientists. "Pluto hasn't changed," planetary

Naming Pluto

Venetia Burney was 11 years old on March 14, 1930. During breakfast that day, her grandfather told her a new planet had been found. Venetia said the planet should be named Pluto. Pluto is the Roman god of the underworld. Her grandfather sent the name to Lowell Observatory, and they agreed with Venetia.

scientist Jean-Luc Margot says. "It's just as exciting."[3]

DISCOVERING THE OTHER DWARF PLANETS

Quaoar lies beyond Pluto's orbit in the Kuiper Belt. It was first sighted from Palomar Observatory in California in 2002. Quaoar is named after a creation god of California's Tongva tribe.

Haumea was discovered in 2003. Two different teams claimed to have found the dwarf planet. Haumea was named after the Hawaiian goddess of fertility and childbirth. In 2017, multiple telescopes tracked Haumea as it passed in front of a star. This is when scientists discovered the dwarf planet's rings.

Palomar Observatory surveyed the outer solar system in October 2003. Astronomers picked through the data and discovered a

The Palomar Observatory is home to the Hale Telescope, which was the largest telescope in the world when it was built.

Pluto-sized object on January 5, 2005. The scientists nicknamed the object Xena after a popular fantasy character.

Scientists debated how to classify the object. This led the IAU to define what a planet is. The organization decided Xena would be a dwarf planet. The IAU then gave Xena its official name, Eris. "Eris is the Greek goddess of discord and strife," says Mike Brown.[4] Brown is a member of the team that discovered Eris. He explains that this name was appropriate because the discovery of Eris caused arguments about the definition of a planet.

The same scientists who discovered Eris discovered Makemake. They observed it in 2005 from the Palomar Observatory. They nicknamed the object Easter Bunny.

In Rapa Nui stories, Makemake is the creator of humanity.

They discovered it just days after Easter. Eventually it was named Makemake. This is the name of the Rapa Nui god of fertility. The Rapa Nui people live on Easter Island in the Pacific Ocean.

CHAPTER THREE

EXPLORING THE DWARF PLANETS

The first spacecraft launched into space in 1957. At first, spacecraft could not travel very far. Early spacecraft went into orbit around Earth and the Moon. As space technology developed, people launched spacecraft on more challenging journeys. Visiting the dwarf planets came with special difficulties. Except for Ceres, the dwarf planets lay beyond the most distant planet

This illustration shows *Pioneer 10* flying by Jupiter in 1973. *Pioneer 10* was the first spacecraft to enter the outer solar system beyond the asteroid belt.

The Hubble Space Telescope orbits Earth once about every 95 minutes.

in the solar system. Reaching these dwarf planets would take a long time.

In the meantime, people studied the dwarf planets using space telescopes. The Hubble Space Telescope (HST) launched into space in 1990. It circles Earth in a low orbit of 320 miles (515 km).

Astronomers control HST remotely from Earth. HST sends back a wide range of images and other data. HST takes images using cameras that see three types of light. Some cameras capture visible light. This is the light people can see. Other cameras capture infrared light. This light has less energy than visible light. Still others capture ultraviolet light. This light has more energy than visible light. Scientists studying Pluto have learned a lot from information gathered by HST.

In 1994, HST took more than a dozen images of Pluto. Some photographs were taken using visible light. Others used ultraviolet light. The photographs detailed almost the entire surface of Pluto. The images revealed several albedo features.

These features are places that reflect light differently than the surrounding area. This can make the features look light or dark. One feature is a group of dark spots. Another is a light polar cap cut in two by a dark band.

This HST image of Pluto was released in 2010. The dwarf planet's great distance from Earth means HST cannot picture its surface in detail.

The HST images helped scientists make a basic map of Pluto. "It's fantastic. Hubble has brought Pluto from a fuzzy, distant dot of light, to a world which we can begin to map . . . . Hubble's view of tiny, distant Pluto is **reminiscent** of looking at Mars through a small telescope," said Alan Stern.[5] Stern works at the Southwest Research Institute's office in Boulder, Colorado.

Atmospheric Distortion

Earth's atmosphere **distorts** distant objects seen through ground-based telescopes. This can make it difficult to observe dwarf planets in the Kuiper Belt. Space telescopes avoid this problem. There is no atmosphere in the way. These telescopes give astronomers more detailed views of distant dwarf planets.

DAWN

Another spacecraft that has gathered information on dwarf planets is *Dawn*. It launched on September 27, 2007. It flew past Mars first. The gravity of this planet put *Dawn* on a path toward the asteroid belt. *Dawn*'s mission was to visit an asteroid called Vesta and the dwarf planet Ceres. The information it gathered would help scientists learn about the formation of the solar system. *Dawn* reached Vesta on July 16, 2011. About a year later, it left for Ceres. It went into orbit around the dwarf planet on March 6, 2015. It gathered information until November 1, 2018, when it ran out of fuel.

Dawn revealed bright spots of salts on Ceres's surface. These salts were left over from evaporated briny water from beneath

Technicians work on the *Dawn* spacecraft before its launch into space.

the surface. Scientists estimate that the water rose to the surface within the past few hundred years. Otherwise, the two spots would have darkened. This happens when they are struck by small meteorites.

Dawn also found evidence of organic material. This material serves as the building blocks of life. This didn't mean life existed on Ceres. But discovering organic material beyond Earth is still exciting for scientists. *Dawn* team member Julie Castillo-Rogez says, "This discovery adds to our understanding of the possible origins of water and organics on Earth."[6]

NEW HORIZONS

New Horizons is a NASA space **probe**. It launched into space on January 19, 2006. Its mission was to learn more about Pluto. It passed the planet Jupiter on its way. This planet's gravity helped send *New Horizons* toward the dwarf planet. After passing Jupiter in 2007, the spacecraft went into electronic hibernation. This means that some of its systems powered down. This saved energy for the long journey ahead.

Finally, in early 2015, *New Horizons* powered back up. Astronomers prepared for its Pluto flyby in July. As the spacecraft passed Pluto, it took lots of photos of the dwarf planet. The photos revealed a large, young, heart-shaped region of ice on Pluto. *New Horizons* also found mountains

Engineers install a part inside *New Horizons*.

made of water ice. Scientists think these mountains might rest on top of buried nitrogen ice. After flying by Pluto, *New Horizons* continued on a path out of the Solar System.

Spacecraft have returned samples from objects beyond Earth before, including this sample from the Moon. Samples from Ceres would be among those taken from the farthest away.

FUTURE MISSIONS

Scientists want to learn more about the dwarf planets. To do this, they are planning to send more spacecraft to them. One of these is *Shensuo*. China's space agency is planning this mission. It would use Jupiter's gravity to fling probes toward the outer solar system. One probe would fly by Quaoar. This would make Quaoar the third dwarf planet to be explored.

NASA is considering sending more spacecraft to Ceres. One proposed mission would do more research on the dwarf planet's organic material. The spacecraft would bring samples of this material back to Earth. Scientists could then study the composition of Ceres in greater detail.

CHAPTER FOUR

MOONS OF THE DWARF PLANETS

More is known about Pluto's moons than those of any other dwarf planet. Pluto has five moons. They are Charon, Nix, Hydra, Kerberos, and Styx. All of these names come from stories of the Roman underworld. These names were chosen because Pluto is the Roman god of the underworld.

When *New Horizons* visited Pluto, it also took photos of the dwarf planet's moons.

This composite image of Pluto's moons displays, from top to bottom, Hydra, Kerberos, Nix, and Styx. Part of Charon's surface is visible at the right of the image.

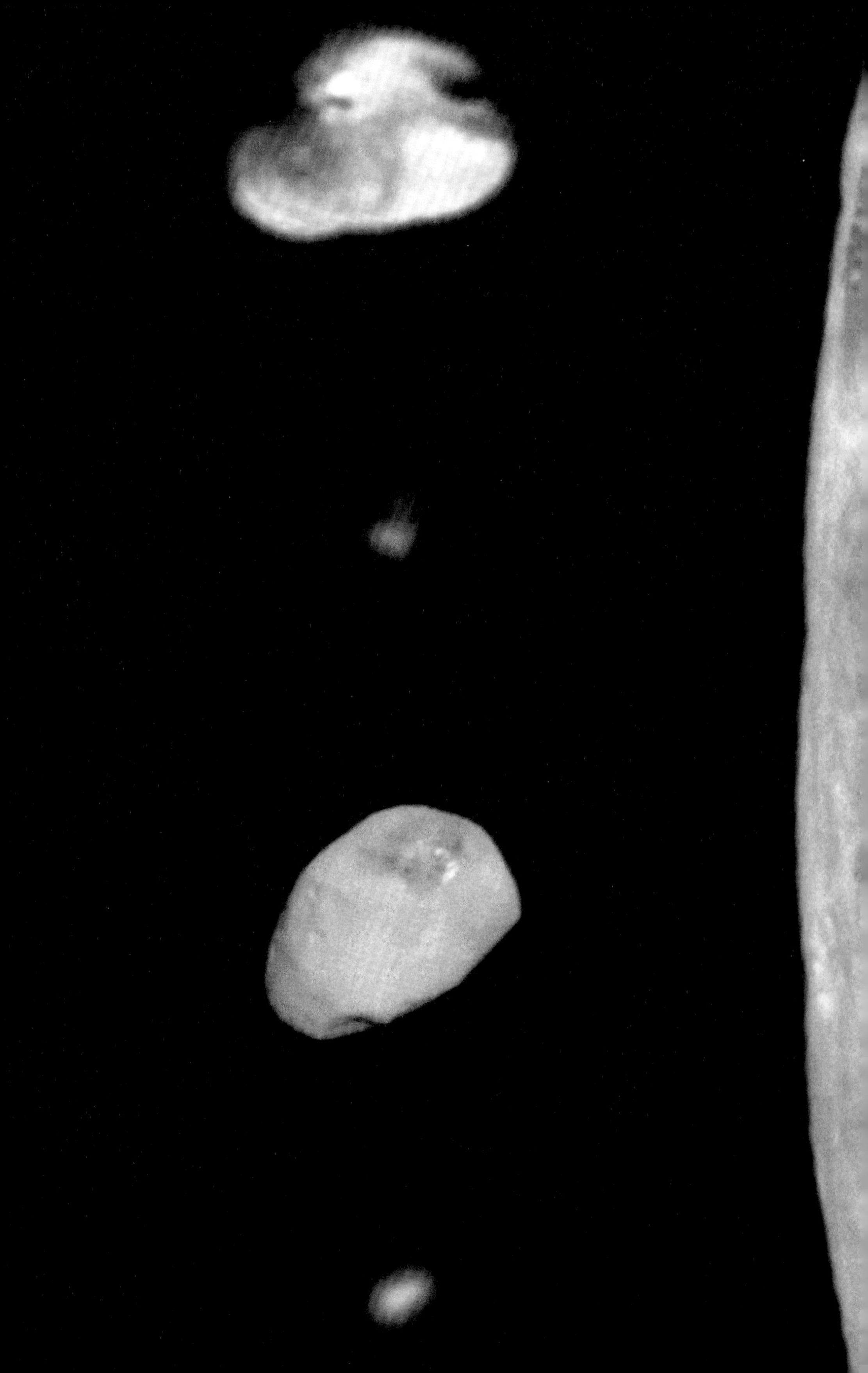

The diameter of Charon is about half that of Pluto, making Charon the largest moon relative to its planet in the solar system.

The probe observed large chasms on Charon. It discovered that the moon's north pole was covered with reddish material. The material may be from Pluto. This indicates that Charon may have struck Pluto in the distant past.

New Horizons also observed Pluto's four smaller moons. It showed that they were spinning faster than they were orbiting Pluto.

This meant that all sides of each moon faced Pluto at one time or another. This is different from how most moons in the solar system orbit. For example, only one side of Earth's Moon faces Earth. This is called tidal locking. It happens when a moon spins exactly once in the time it takes to complete an orbit.

Ted Stryk worked on the *New Horizons* team. He was surprised by the photos of Pluto's moons. He said, "Before last week, Hydra was just a faint point of light, so it's a surreal experience to see it become an actual place."[7]

OTHER MOONS

Haumea has two known moons. Both were discovered in 2005. Namaka, the inner moon, is named after a water spirit in Hawaiian mythology. It takes Namaka 18 days to orbit Haumea.

Hi‘aka is the outer moon. It is named after the goddess of the island of Hawaii. Hi‘aka orbits Haumea every 49 days. It is covered in water ice. Infrared images revealed this ice. Scientists think this moon may have once been part of Haumea.

Eris has a small moon called Dysnomia. This moon is named after Eris's daughter, the demon goddess of lawlessness. It has a nearly circular orbit that takes about 16 days. The moon was discovered in 2005. Astronomers were observing Eris from the Keck Observatory in Mauna Kea, Hawaii. They were using a new instrument that gave them a more detailed view into

This illustration shows Haumea, its ring, and its two moons.

the Kuiper Belt. They were able to see the faint Dysnomia orbiting Eris.

The James Webb Space Telescope has also observed Dysnomia. It found that Eris and Dysnomia are tidally locked to each other. Typically, only one body is tidally locked to the other. Scientists suspect that Dysnomia slowed down Eris's rotation. This caused the dwarf planet to become tidally locked to its moon.

Dysnomia orbits Eris in faint sunlight in this NASA illustration.

This fact taught scientists about the composition of Eris. Francis Nimmo is an interplanetary scientist at the University of California, Santa Cruz. "Dysnomia is pretty small. It's a fairly wimpy moon," he says. "And so in order for it to have spun Eris down, it turns out that Eris must have been pretty squishy. And we have a way of measuring the squishiness of

Eris basically."[8] Nimmo and other scientists think Eris is made of rock and an icy layer that was once relatively warm.

In 2007, the team involved in the discovery of Quaoar announced that a moon had been discovered orbiting the dwarf planet. They named it Weywot. Weywot is a sky god and the son of Quaoar. The scientists think Weywot broke off Quaoar when the dwarf planet struck another object.

James Webb Space Telescope

The James Webb Space Telescope launched into space on December 25, 2021. It does not orbit Earth. Instead, it orbits the Sun. It observes using infrared light. It was designed to detect distant objects. Scientists hope it will help them identify additional dwarf planets.

PROVISIONAL MOONS

Makemake has one **provisional** moon. Provisional moons are moons that do not yet have official names. They are given temporary names. Makemake's moon is called S/2015 (136472) 1. *S* means it is a satellite or moon. The next number is the year it was discovered. The number in parentheses is a unique number given to Makemake. And the last number means it was the first moon of Makemake discovered that year.

Makemake's moon is fainter than the dwarf planet. It was identified in April 2015 by a special camera on HST. This camera allows astronomers to see faint objects near bright ones. The moon is about 13,000 miles (21,000 km) from the

This NASA illustration of the Makemake system was produced shortly after the discovery of Makemake's moon.

dwarf planet. Its diameter is about 100 miles (160 km) across.

Although dwarf planets are not true planets, they remain interesting to scientists. Astronomers still have a lot to learn about the known dwarf planets. And new dwarf planets may be discovered in the future.

GLOSSARY

astronomical

relating to the study of space

atmosphere

gases that surround a planet

axis of rotation

an imaginary line running through a planet's poles around which the planet spins

distorts

changes or alters the shape or appearance of something

evaporated

became a gas from a liquid

observatory

a place with a telescope and other scientific tools that are used to study space

probe

a device sent to space that gathers information

provisional

temporary until something more official is chosen

reminiscent

reminding one of something else

SOURCE NOTES

INTRODUCTION: SEEING CERES

1. Quoted in "Mystery Solved: Bright Areas on Ceres Come From Salty Water Below," *NASA*, August 10, 2020. www.nasa.gov.

CHAPTER ONE: THE DWARF PLANETS

2. "When Does a Dwarf Planet Become a Planet?" *YouTube*, uploaded by AstroPhil, September 2, 2022. www.youtube.com.

CHAPTER TWO: DISCOVERING THE DWARF PLANETS

3. Quoted in Joanna Thompson, "Why Is Pluto Not Considered a Planet?" *LiveScience*, November 13, 2024. www.livescience.com.

4. Quoted in Nola Taylor Tillman, "Eris: The First Dwarf Planet," *Space.com*, July 10, 2019. www.space.com.

CHAPTER THREE: EXPLORING THE DWARF PLANETS

5. Quoted in "Hubble Reveals Surface of Pluto for First Time," *NASA Hubblesite*, March 7, 1996. https://hubblesite.org.

6. Quoted in Elizabeth Landau, "*Dawn* Discovers Evidence for Organic Material on Ceres," *Jet Propulsion Laboratory*, February 16, 2017. www.jpl.nasa.gov.

CHAPTER FOUR: MOONS OF THE DWARF PLANETS

7. Quoted in "*New Horizons* Unveils Pluto and Its Moons," *RocketSTEM*, July 15, 2015. www.rocketstem.org.

8. Quoted in John Wenz, "A Moon Helps to Uncover Strange Solar System Body Eris," *Astronomy*, November 20, 2023. www.astronomy.com.

FOR FURTHER RESEARCH

BOOKS

Yvette LaPierre, *The Asteroid Belt.* BrightPoint Press, 2022.

Christine Marie Layton, *Beyond the Solar System.* BrightPoint Press, 2022.

Gail Radley, *The Space Encyclopedia*. Abdo Publishing, 2023.

INTERNET SOURCES

"Space Shorts: What Is a Dwarf Planet?" *Jet Propulsion Laboratory*, September 25, 2024. www.jpl.nasa.gov.

Tricia Talbert, "NASA's New Horizons to Continue Exploring Outer Solar System," *NASA*, September 29, 2023. www.nasa.gov.

"Why Is Pluto No Longer a Planet?" *Library of Congress*, February 25, 2025. www.loc.gov.

WEBSITES

NASA: Dwarf Planets
https://science.nasa.gov/dwarf-planets

This NASA website on the dwarf planets includes links to videos and articles. It also discusses the controversy surrounding the definition of a dwarf planet.

NASA: Eyes on the Solar System
https://eyes.nasa.gov

On NASA's Eyes on the Solar System website, visitors can explore a simulation of the solar system. The simulation includes the positions of spacecraft associated with active NASA missions.

The Schools' Observatory
www.schoolsobservatory.org

The Schools' Observatory guides visitors on how to observe the night sky. The website also has information about career paths in astronomy.

INDEX

IMAGE CREDITS

Cover: © NASA
5: © NASA
7: © Regina Mitchell-Ryall & Jerry Cannon/NASA
8: © NASA
10: © NASA
13: © NASA
14: © NASA
16: © NASA
17: © NASA
19: © NASA
21: © Kevin Gill/Flickr
23: © European Space Agency/Science Source
25: © Juliasuena/Shutterstock Images
27: © Vivvi Smak/Shutterstock Images
29: © Science Source
30: © nivium/Flickr
33: © Denys/Wikimedia Commons
35: © Don Couch/Alamy
37: © NASA
38: © NASA
40: © NASA
43: © NASA
45: © NASA
46: © NASA
49: © NASA
50: © NASA
53: © Mark Garlick/Science Source
54: © NASA
57: © NASA

ABOUT THE AUTHOR

Sue Bradford Edwards is a nonfiction author who writes from her home office in Missouri. Her favorite topics include social sciences and sciences including astronomy. Her favorite observatory is the University of Texas McDonald Observatory in Fort Davis, Texas.